THE DOUGLAS

APPROACH

THE DOUGLAS

APPROACH

Conquering by Building Resilience

JOSHALINE DOUGLAS

ISBN-13: 978-1987620375

ISBN-10: 1987620372

All italics in the Bible texts were added by the author for emphasis.

National Foster Youth Institute (2017). 51 Useful aging out of foster care statistics. Retrieved https://www.nfyi.org/51-useful-aging-out-of-foster-care-statistics-social-race-media/

Bulk Sales

Books are available at special discounst for bulk purchase. For more information please email joshaline.douglas@gmail.com

Printed in the United States of America

Book design by Joshaline Douglas

Cover Photographer Robert Dickerson | @91nephotography

DEDICATION

This book is dedicated to every foster child who believed they couldn't. I'm determined to defeat every statistic society has set for us. To the person that continues to strive to master the art of resilience.

May my story of truth empower you to discover your purpose and stretch your faith, regardless of the challenges life brings.

And most Importantly, remember you are resilient!

◆

"I believe dreams were not given to us just to sit on, but they were given purposefully, for us to make them a reality"
-Joshaline Douglas

"Be the change you wish to see in the world"
-Mahatma Gandhi

"Resilience is being able to overcome the unexpected"
-Jamais Cascio

ACKNOWLEDGMENTS

I never imagined this day to come. I somewhat doubted myself beyond anything else. I thought writing a book was the most intimidating thing to accomplish. I always had the dream of becoming a published author. I'd been prophesied to on many occasions, but it never manifested until I decided to take on the challenge. Yes, writing a book is a rigorous process, but that's anything worth having in this life. Through hard work and commitment, I'm able to finally say, "I'm an author".

First I would like to give an honor to God for giving me the tenacity to achieve such demanding task. Finding an effective balance between being a mother, school, and work was tough, but I serve a sovereign God. He did it just for me, and I owe it all to him.

To my greatest creation Noah, you came into my life at the right time and have only changed my life for the better. You're my reason why and I'll always strive to be the best mother I can be for you.

To my siblings, thank you for beating the odds. I'm so proud of you all (Michelle, Antonio, and Albert). Although life hasn't always been the greatest, you've created the best life for yourselves. I will always love you!

To my biological mother Tammy, you've given me the greatest gift and that is life. I could never repay you.

To my dear mother Sonya, you're my super hero. You took on a significant role as my mother figure. You've always gone over and beyond to ensure I have everything I need and most of what I want. You've supported me every step of the way. Thanks for all you do for me and Noah.

To my Aunt Julia, Uncle Herman, Aunt Dianne, and Uncle Bubby, thank you for believing in me. Your support has been unwavering. Your encouragement has pushed me all the more to make my dreams a reality.

To the greatest social worker of all time Ms. Fantasia, you have paved the way for me. I've learned so much from watching you. You've been a wonderful role model in my life and a true inspiration. Thanks for allowing me to invade your space and learn from you.

Special thanks to my best friend of eleven years. Larry you're the greatest friend, supporter, and encourager ever. You've always been honest and consistent. You've motivated me to chase my dreams like never before. You've challenged me to maximize my full potential; often potential I can't see in myself. You're a true gift from God.

To my best friend Venikia, thanks for being a helping hand to Noah and I. You've always been the friend to listen and understand. You give me the freedom to be myself. You've shed positivity during some of the darkest times of my life. Although we don't always see eye to eye on everything, I appreciate our endless conversations because it has challenged me to grow in imperative areas of my life.

To my teaching parents The Richburg's, you've not only helped to structure my foundation, but you both have been spiritual parents, guiders, and advisors. Thank you for your continuous support and prayers.

To my dear friend Jasmine, you've always had an open

door policy when it came to me and Noah. Your continuous words of affirmation give me a constant reminder of who God created me to be. Your words have given me all the more drive to live my best life.

To Noah's God mother Aquanetta, thank you for your unwavering support. You took the role of a God parent with no questions. I appreciate your authenticity. You're truly the peanut butter to my jelly (*smile*).

To the best academic counselor Ms. Macfoy, thank you for taking time to get to know me. You've welcomed me and Noah into your family with open arms. You're the perfect example of excellence. You desire the best for your students and make every effort to ensure their educational experience is nothing less. I wouldn't have made it without you.

Lastly, but certainly not least The Boys and Girls Homes of North Carolina, there's no way I could ever repay this organization for all it has done for me. You all have supported me in every way imaginable, gave me the proper exposure to networking opportunities, and were truly the light in a dark place of my life. Words cannot express my gratitude.

To my readers, thank you for taking the time to read my

story. I pray that it impacts your life in a major way. There are millions of books you could be reading right now, but you landed here. Awesome choice! So, thank you.

THE DOUGLAS

APPROACH

CONTENTS

INTRODUCTION

Resilience is the art of bouncing back. When we become resilient, adversity becomes the catalyst for growth. Adversity has a way of breaking us down, just to build us right back up. Sometimes in life, we question our ability to overcome situations because of what we're experiencing in the moment. However, I challenge you to open your mind up to new ways of thinking. **TRULY CONQUERING** is a mind set. When we learn to change our perspective, we then change our reality. Conquering is not limited to exceeding the expectations of others. It's thoroughly becoming connected with who we are as individuals, to reach the level of self-actualization.

I can truly say at this point in my life, I've conquered and thoroughly pursued my dreams. Although nowhere near where

I desire, I'm prayerful of what's to come. Coming from what seemed like a dead end road, I maximized my full potential. This has led to much of my success today.

I'm an ordinary girl from Durham, North Carolina, who has an extraordinary story, as others would say. I was initially raised in a single parent home with two of my siblings before entering into the foster care system. My youngest brother remained in the care of his father to avoid being taken into custody.

My biological mother struggled most of her life. She was born in poverty and wasn't exposed to anything different. She also grew up in the foster care system. Foster care was a generational cycle for my immediate family. Therefore, I was determined to break the cycle of poverty, lack of educational attainment, and allowing life's barriers to stop me from getting everything that God had destined. There were many bumps in the road, but I committed to my success.

Through the years, I've learned that the key to making my dreams a reality is having a vision, creating a plan, and executing. In order to effectively execute the plan, our minds must to be transformed to achieve the goals that are set. It means changing our mindset from instant gratification, to goal orientation. Every day keep striving, keep believing, and **STAY FOCUSED!** Believe it or not, it's easy to get off track. When we do, we push ourselves further away from our destiny.

I believe dreams were not given to us just to sit on, but they were given purposefully, for us to make them a reality. Every day is a new day to do something that sets your soul on fire. Find that thing you're passionate about and go after it as if your life depended on it. All things may not seem to be working in your favor, but each challenge in life brings new perspective. Romans 8:28 (NKJV) states "And we know that all things work together for good to those that love God, who are called according to *His* purpose." God's timing is always perfect. You will find that your passion is connected to your purpose. Don't ever give up on that, keep fighting as I did!

There's no way I can be an agent for change, if I'm not first honest about my personal life. I say this to say; in this book I share many of my challenges and triumphs in the most authentic way because my truth has the potential to help someone else. So come --- take this journey with me on how I've conquered by building resilience. <u>**WARNING**</u>**: I say, "At least, that's what I thought" numerous times throughout the book (*smile*).**

CHAPTER ONE

ENTERING FOSTER CARE

I don't ever remember living with my biological parents. From what I was told, we lived with my biological mother when we were infants. My father was never present in my life due to incarceration. According to my childhood record, my mother reported to The Department of Social Services (DSS) that she wasn't mentally or financially stable to care for us. My mother never officially graduated high school, so she struggled with finding steady employment. She also believed to not have the mental capacity to work in any other role, except being a janitor. With four children and limited credentials there was no way she could take care of us effectively.

Before we were taken directly into custody, DSS gave my mom the opportunity to utilize kinship care. Kinship care is the preferred resource for children who must be removed from their birth parents. It's known to maintain the children's connections with their families. Therefore, DSS reached out to my grandmother in Charlotte, North Carolina to see if she would be interested in keeping us. She agreed. So, we prepared to move from Durham, North Carolina to Charlotte, North Carolina. During our transition, my grandmother had several guy friends that would come in and out of her home. I then realized our home was the local "trap house". A place where drugs were bought, sold, and produced.

One guy in particular we called him "Stover", he was the neighborhood drug dealer. Whatever you needed, he had it. **TRUST ME**. He also was a drug addict, which made sense because he was his own "plug" (a *drug connection)*. I remember there being a corner store up the street from my grandmother's home. My siblings and I would ride our bikes there and see him smoking and drinking behind the store. I never knew his drug of choice until years later. When I did find out, I was utterly disturbed. His drug of choice was crack cocaine. He eventually introduced my grandmother to the drug, and she too became addicted. There were many nights my siblings and I were left home alone to fend for ourselves. My brother was our protector. If anything went down, he was the first one to fight. My sister was more so the nurturer. She made sure we ate and were prepared for school the next day. Believe it or not, I maintained the cleanliness of the house. Our house was infested with roaches, but I tried my best to make our house a home.

There was also a lack of food in the home. Most of time, we ate what we could find, whether that was ketchup and mayonnaise sandwiches, cold hotdogs, or if you were anything like me, slices of cheese. This was no way to live. However when someone is addicted to drugs, it consumes their life and affects their better judgment.

There were even times we came home from school and my grandmother and Stover would be assaulting one another. One night in particular, they got in an altercation that led to them stabbing each other. My grandmother screamed for us to come and help her. When I ran into the room, she was bleeding uncontrollably. She told one of us to immediately call the police. The neighborhood we lived in, it was normal to go outside and see an officer lurking around. So when we did go, there was an officer driving down our street. We ran the officer down to tell him what was going on. Stover went to jail that night, but we all knew he would return because getting into fights and calling the police was a norm.

My siblings and I were exposed to substance abuse and domestic violence at a young age. As time went on, our school became concerned with our well-being due to our outward appearance. We would wear dirty clothes, our hair was not kept appropriately, and we'd go to school hungry.

I began to see a therapist during school hours. I revealed to her everything that was going on at home. Within that same week, I came home and found out my grandmother was arrested for possession of an illegal substance with the intent to sell. My siblings and I stayed with the neighbors. I would ask them questions like, "When is my grandmother coming home? Or Is she okay?" They would tell me that she would return soon.

A couple of days had passed and there were no signs of my grandmother. Instead police showed up to our house. The neighbors walked across the street to see what they needed. The officers said, "We have a warrant to search the home." The neighbors gave the officers access to the home. At the time, I didn't know why they needed to search the home, but years later I was told it was searched for illegal substances. Crack cocaine was found in the home, and a child protective services (CPS) report was filed.

Saturday, April 15, 2002 at approximately 4:16pm, a day I remember so clearly. My siblings and I were preparing to leave with the neighbors. A white car with a sign that read, "Mecklenburg County DSS" pulled up in front of the neighbor's house. The social worker walked up to the van that we were in and said, "I'm looking for Michelle, Joshaline, and Antonio." I was the first one to speak up. "That's us" I replied. The social worker said, "You all need to come with me." We proceeded to get out of the van. My sister and brother began crying. I felt as if I was the strongest one during the entire process. The neighbors looked as if they knew what was happening.

Once the social worker got us in the car, she explained that her role was to keep children safe. She also explained that we would be going to live in a foster home. I was six years old at the time. I'd always envisioned foster care to be like the movie *Annie*. If you're not familiar with the movie, Annie lived in an orphanage with about seven to ten female residents. The orphanage was run by a mean lady, Ms. Hannigan. She treated the girls as if they were slaves. While riding to our foster home that was the only thing I could imagine. The possibility of scrubbing floors, being yelled at on a daily basis, and living in an unhappy environment scared me.

I hugged my sister and brother during the ride. I told them that everything was going to be okay. I asked the social worker, "Will we be staying together?" She said, "No, boys and girls aren't allowed to live in the same home." I was extremely hurt, and my brother was devastated.

We arrived at the foster home where my brother would be living. My sister and I said our goodbyes. It was the worst experience imaginable. We were together since birth and all of a sudden we were taken away from each another. It felt as if we were being punished for being in a neglectful situation. After all, we were just children. It wasn't our fault.

Visual Moment

Close your eyes. Imagine holding on to something you love dearly and all of a sudden it vanishes. How would you feel? What would you do? How would you react? This is how I felt when we were separated.

After leaving my brother, we were in route to me and my sister's foster home. When we arrived, I was amazed at the beautiful home. The social worker walked us to the door and rang the door bell. When the door opened, I saw two women. It was one African American woman and one Caucasian woman. They greeted me and my sister with a warm smile and a loving hug. They introduced themselves as Lisa and Lonnie. Both of them wanted to know if we were ready to see our room. My sister and I both said, "Yes!" in excitement.

When they walked us to our room my eyes lit up. The room was painted blue with glowing stars and moon décor in the ceiling. We also had moon and star comforter sets, our own personalized robes, and we even had our own bathroom and television. I was elated! I never had a room with décor, my own bathroom and television, or a mother who gave out free hugs at the drop of a dime. In that moment I felt free, genuinely loved, and like a true kid.

After viewing our room, the social worker gave me and my sister a hug goodbye. She let us know that she was on the case temporarily, and we would be receiving a new social worker. From that day forward, my life completely changed.

CHAPTER TWO

THE ODDS OF LFE

The new social worker came to visit us at our foster home. She introduced herself as Ms. Staton. She told us that she would be taking over our case from that point on. The Department of Social Services goal is to always consider family when it comes to the permanency of a child, to avoid placing children in the foster care system. They like to do what's in the best interest of the child (ren). Therefore, Ms. Staton reached out to our family members who could potentially take us in. She was able to locate my cousin Maurice. He lived in Columbia, South Carolina. He agreed to take us in, so we wouldn't be separated. After about a year of him taking imperative classes, completing paperwork, and background checks, his home was finally approved.

Moving out of my first foster home was tough. We went on family vacations, had the best holidays, and never missed a WNBA Charlotte Sting's game. They had exposed us to positive things we'd never experienced before. Most importantly, they taught us how to be children because we were used to being the parental figures. I'll never forget those sweet ladies. However, it was time to move forward.

In the summer of 2003, we moved in with my cousin. Everything was progressing well. I enjoyed seeing my sibling's every day. I was enrolled in the fourth grade at Piney Grove Elementary School. My siblings and I were a part of the after school program. Me and my sister's favorite after school counselor was Ms. Phinisha. One day Ms. Phinisha announced that she was leaving the program for another opportunity. Therefore, she planned a going away sleepover and invited all of her favorite students. My sister and I attended the sleep over. I met Ms. Phinisha's mom, Ms. Sonya. Who would've known I'd be calling her "mom" today? There was an instant connection, and I never lost contact with her since that day. I completed my fourth grade year successfully at Piney Grove and was promoted to the fifth grade.

Back to Charlotte AGAIN!

. . . .

In the summer of 2004, everything took a dramatic turn. My sister was moved back to Charlotte, North Carolina due to conflict between her and my cousin. She couldn't seem to get along with him. She was angry and had every reason to be. Ms. Staton began to question whether a male figure could appropriately parent an eight year old female. She believed it was necessary for a female figure to guide me into womanhood in the years to come. The final decision was made for me to move back to Charlotte, North Carolina with my sister. My brother remained with my cousin.

When I moved back to Charlotte, North Carolina, my brother and I lost contact because we no longer lived in the same home. I resented Ms. Staton because it was not my desire to move out of my cousin's home. Although my experience in foster care wasn't horrible, I didn't want to go back. I desired to be with my biological family. This was the catalyst to my down spiral of behaviors.

I began the fifth grade at J.W. Harris Academy. I was suspended from school on a consistent basis for talking back, fighting, and not following instructions. This was only the beginning of my behavior issues. It soon got much worse. I also began disrupting my foster home placement. My foster mom could no longer manage my behaviors. I was moved to a different foster home during the middle of my fifth grade year, causing me and my sister to separate once more. I was at my new foster home for about six months before DSS considered family again.

This time they decided to contact my maternal aunt and uncle. They agreed to take us in their care. They resided in Durham, North Carolina along with their two daughters. I always questioned if they would be able to manage all four of us, but only time would tell. Even through my behavior issues, I completed the fifth grade successfully. It was time for me to transition to my aunt and uncle's home.

Welcome to Durham

* * * *

In the summer of 2005, my sister and I moved to Durham, North Carolina. My aunt and uncle didn't stay in the best of neighborhood, but we made the best of the environment. Coming from a foster home that was in a prestige area, to living in what people referred to as, "The hood" was surely a culture shock. However, I adapted well. I'm not sure if that was in my best interest because I began engaging in things I normally wouldn't entertain.

When I began making friends in the neighborhood, I quickly realized the kids around me were well experienced. I'm speaking in terms of things that "should've" been unfamiliar to an eleven year old. The kids that I met had already experienced sexual intercourse, smoked illegal substances, and were apart of street gangs. That gives you a clear idea about the youth population who lived in our neighborhood.

Those things were out of the norm for me. I believed getting suspended from school made me a hard core girl, but apparently that was nothing compared to my peers. So of course, I desired to fit in with the rest of my counter parts. My sister and I gave ourselves the street name, "The New Jersey Girls", knowing we were really not from New Jersey. We came up with the name because there was a family who lived a couple of buildings down from us that were from New York. We referred to them as the "The New York Girls".

A lot of events took place at my aunt and uncle's home. I got into my first fight, jumped by a gang of girls, physically assaulted by my uncle, had my first sexual experience, and was put out of the house by my aunt. I was only eleven years old. I couldn't imagine the typical eleven year old taking on that much trauma. Therefore, our stay at my aunt and uncle's was shortly lived.

Once my sister and I were kicked out of the house, she filed a CPS report. She said, "It's too much drama here. I was previously in a fight with my uncle, and my aunt put me and my sister out of the house." The next day, a CPS worker came out to the home and interviewed everyone. Our case was screened in as an investigative assessment due to the presented allegations in the report. The case was substantiated because new evidence was presented in the report, resulting in an immediate removal from the home.

It was found that my uncle had prior sexual offenses on a minor, which contributed to our immediate removal. You may be wondering, "Why were they moved there in the first place if the uncle had prior sexual offenses?" My only answer is someone "dropped the ball" when it came to the appropriate background check. My cousins were moved to a kinship placement in Charlotte, North Carolina. My aunt and uncle ended up divorcing following these events. So, there I was entering the foster care system a third time. People say, "The third time's a charm."

My 3rd Time Around

. . . .

When I arrived at my first foster home in Durham, North Carolina, I was angry. I hated the foster home because I felt like she was only doing it for the money. Additionally, I had to switch schools because I was no longer in the same district. I was switched from Chewning Middle School to Githens Middle School. My sister and I would stay home alone after school. We would fight like cats and dogs, but maybe even worse (*smile*). Our safety became a major concern. At our child and family team meeting, it was recommended that we no longer live together due to the best interest of our safety. During this meeting, we met our new social worker. She introduced herself as Ms. Sarah. After our initial introduction, everything... and I do mean everything went downhill.

When my sister was moved, my behaviors regressed. We didn't keep in contact or have visits with each other, so our relationship declined. I ended up being moved to a different foster home, resulting in another change of schools. I began attending Neal Middle School. This particular foster home didn't last long either. The foster parent and I clashed on numerous occasions, but I was able to remain in the same school. I was on my third school and foster home in just a couple of months. I was surely on a roll. My social worker recommended a higher level of care.

When I came back into foster care, I lived in a traditional foster home. Due to the multiple interrupted placements in such a short time frame, Ms. Sarah believed a therapeutic foster home would accommodate my behavioral needs. A therapeutic foster home was considered a level two placement. Foster parents were trained on crisis intervention and how to appropriately respond to behavior challenges. So, I was moved to a therapeutic foster home.

This particular foster home was different from the rest. My foster mom, Ms. Reedy had a passion for working with children. She worked in a daycare full-time, so she was well equipped with taking care of children. She desired to see me excel. She saw potential in me that I hadn't seen in myself. Ms. Reedy allowed me to participate in extracurricular activities, which gave me the outlet to express my aggression in a positive way. I began seeing a therapist, taking psychiatric medications, and attending a day treatment program that taught me self-help skills to appropriately manage my anger. Although unsatisfied with the eleven psychiatric diagnoses, I remained humble because there was no way I was allowing labels to define me.

During my stay at Ms. Reedy's, we attended church regularly. I do mean **regularly**. I'm talking every revival, pastor's aide service, or bible study. You name it, and we were there. I experienced my first spiritual encounter. I was raised in a Christian household, although not so Christian things happened. So, I had somewhat of a reverence for God. But this particular time, I felt a genuine connection with him, something I'd never experienced before. So, I desired a deeper relationship with him. I believed he knew all I was going through, and he would fix everything soon. I guess soon, wasn't soon enough.

I began missing several days of school because I refused to go. When I did go, I would intentionally do things to be suspended. I was eventually expelled from school due to my excessive suspensions. I was only allowed back to take my end of course examinations.

I felt like my life was totally different from the students

around me. It seemed as if, I was the only who didn't live with their biological family. I didn't feel like a regular kid. I couldn't do things as my peers did such as attend sleepovers, hang out at the mall, or go to the movies with my friends. Everything had to be approved by my social worker, which meant parents were subjected to background checks and home studies to ensure I was in a safe environment. A lot of the parents didn't want to go through that process because DSS had to get in their personal business. So, I spent most of my time at home bored. I guess that time alone paid off.

Through the multiple foster homes, school changes, and being expelled, I still managed to complete the sixth grade successfully. I wasn't proud of my behaviors, but this was a prime example of resilience. I was thrilled to know I passed my end of course examinations. Academics were never an issue for me. It was always my behavior.

It was the summer of 2006. I was enrolled in summer camp, which was a part of my day treatment. The directors of the program were like fathers. They treated me like their own. They saw greatness inside of me, but I hadn't discovered it myself. This is the problem in most of our lives.

Tip #1: Once we thoroughly become connected with who we are, then we can truly conquer.

The summer went by so fast. When the school year came back around, I expected to attend the public school. After being expelled, I'm not sure why I assumed such a thing. However, I was in for a rude awakening. My foster parent told me I would be attending the alternative school. Lakeview is the alternative school in Durham, North Carolina. There were two locations for Lakeview. One location was for short-term students, and the other location was for long-term students who may need additional emotional or behavioral support. I was placed at the long-term location.

When I began the school year, it was so different from a public school. I had to walk through a metal detector every day, put my belongings in a cubby, and adhere to a strict dress code. You couldn't tell me I wasn't being institutionalized. The school even had a "turn around room" that looked like a jail cell. I felt like a criminal, who hadn't committed a crime... as of yet.

To top things off, Ms. Sarah had the nerve to make another recommendation for placement. That was a "double whammy" for me. So not only was I attending an alternative school, but she was recommending a higher level of care. Once again, her decision was merely based off my multiple placement changes, being expelled from school, and my continuous behavior issues. She believed a group home would be able to effectively manage my behavior versus a therapeutic foster home. Her recommendation was granted. However, she didn't allow me to move during the school year to avoid the move impeding on my academics. Therefore, she waited until I completed the seventh grade.

I ended the school year successfully. Of course, there were behavior concerns, but overall I performed well. I made a three on my math end of course examination and a four on my english end of course examination. A four is the highest score anyone could earn. I was thrilled, but reality set in, and I was off to my first group home.

CHAPTER THREE

THE GROUP HOME SERIES

"Welcome to Kinder Care Group Home!" I can still hear Mrs. Jane's voice so clearly. Mrs. Jane was the group home owner and director. She seemed to be a nice woman who had my best interest at heart. She made sure she attended every child and family team meeting. She was thoroughly involved when it came to the upkeep of the home and resident concerns. She had proved to be a woman of her word. She devoted her efforts to the success of her residents. I thought, "Maybe a group home isn't so bad after all."

Everything had seemed to be going well, until the day I got into a disagreement with one of the group home staff members. I didn't believe the situation was handled correctly.

Granted being argumentative with staff was never appropriate. I would consider myself a "hot head" back then, but I rationalized well. In this particular situation, I didn't believe I deserved consequences. We both were disrespectful to each other, but I was the only one who was rendered consequences. From that day forward, I didn't look at Mrs. Jane in the same light.

However, there was one staff member that I did favor. Her name was Ms. Hershey. She really cared about the residents at the group home. She treated us as if we were her own children. She gave us sound advice, held us accountable, and gave us praise for our successes. If I couldn't go to anyone else with my problems, she was always open to listen. I also had a favorite resident. Her name was Anna. She was like my big sister because once my biological sister and I separated, our relationship declined. I didn't have anyone else to discuss personal matters with, so I confided in her. She was able to understand my point of view because she had a similar background. Anna and I had our share of disagreements, but we understood the importance of forgiveness.

One Thursday evening, Anna and I discussed running away from the group home. We didn't have a plan… as of yet. We were tired of living in a structured environment and not being able to do the things we wanted. Our bedtime was 9pm, we had thirty minutes a day allotted for phone time (*I loved talking on the phone by the way*), and we couldn't even hang out with our friends. **What teenager wouldn't want to run away?** Friday evening arrived, and we continued to discuss running away. This time we had a plan. We were going to take the group home van and go for a spin. We didn't care about the potential consequences to our decisions. All we thought about was escaping our miserable reality.

Saturday afternoon, we executed the plan. Staff was asleep at the time (*they weren't supposed to be*), and the other residents were in their rooms. We were able to confiscate the vehicle keys, climb out of Anna's window, and leave in the van. We had no place in mind to go, so we cruised around the city. It felt good to be free of supervision for a **few hours**. When staff awoke, they reported the vehicle stolen and that two residents were missing.

According to Mrs. Jane, she had some of her colleagues looking for us as well. We were found three hours later by Anna's mentor. Her mentor called the police, and we were arrested at the scene. I was charged with possession of a stolen vehicle and grand larceny, at the age of thirteen. I felt my life was over. How could I ever move forward in life with two felonies? I was taken back to the group home and Anna went to jail due to prior convictions.

Tip #2: Never make emotional decisions, it will cost you.

My first appearance was scheduled two weeks after the incident occurred. Mrs. Jane was there for moral support. Although she had every reason to be angry, she wasn't. She was more so concerned with our safety. She told me to take the incident as a learning curve.

When my court date arrived, I was beyond nervous. Mrs. Jane transported me to the court house. I'd never been diagnosed with anxiety before, but in that moment I began sweating, breathing heavily, and my thoughts were racing. When my case was called, I came forward. The prosecutor presented the case to the judge. She recommended the maximum sentence, which was to serve time in the juvenile detention center. However when you're a child of the king, there is something called "**The favor of God!**" He's a faithful God, even when we aren't faithful.

The judge looked at me and said, "I believe this was bad judgment on your part, but you're an honor roll student. I'm going to decrease the two felony charges to a misdemeanor." I hadn't done anything to deserve such favor, but I was grateful. I could've shouted for joy in that moment, but I held it together for the sake of being in the court room. She added, "You're ordered to serve a twelve-month probationary period, with monthly visits to see your probation officer, and you must attend a girls group as restitution." If didn't adhere to the guidelines of my probation, I would be ordered to serve time in the juvenile detention center. When I left court, I felt relieved. I desired to do better for myself. So, I decided that day I was going to "try my best" to stay on track.

I was in the eighth grade, attending the alternative school, excelling academically per usual, and adhering to the guidelines of my probation. I was doing so well that I made it to the highest level (*Platinum*) at the alternative school. I was offered a transitional period. During the transition, students were allowed to take courses at the public school. If students performed well, they were able to transition to public school full-time. This was big deal for me. I desired to attend public school again. However, this had to be approved by Ms.Sarah. I knew that if the decision was left up to her, she wouldn't approve it. I wasn't the best client to work with, but it seemed as if she was against anything positive happening in my life.

School officials called for a child and family team meeting to develop a plan. When I arrived at the meeting, aI noticed my social worker wasn't there. It wasn't like her not to show up. As the meeting continued, I realized a new social worker was there in her place. I was excited because **maybe** she would do a better job than Ms.Sarah. She only came around when things were going bad, but I wanted her to be around during the good times as well. To top things off, she didn't tell me she was resigning. I found out after the meeting, but I could care less either way.

Following the meeting, the new social worker introduced herself as Ms. Fantasia. She was an adoptions social worker. She congratulated me on my transition and was happy to be approving something positive. I asked, "Am I up for adoption?" She said, "Yes, your mother's parental rights were terminated."

The court system had given my mom several chances to comply, but a man was more important than her children.

However, I was excited to be up for adoption because it gave me a better chance at finding a forever family. I told her about my experiences with Ms. Sarah. She apologized on her behalf, and told me that she would give her best effort. I was skeptical of the relationship, but I trusted the process.

Best friend

. . . .

The first day of classes began the fall of 2007. I began my transition at Carrington Middle School. I took my math and english courses at the public school, and my science and history courses were taken at the alternative school. I remember being escorted to my math class by the guidance counselor. All I could think about is how liberating it felt to walk in a building without feel criminalized. We arrived at my classroom. I was introduced to my new teacher and classmates. As I was walking to my desk, I noticed an African American guy, with straight back braids, who wore glasses. You couldn't miss him because he sat right by the door. I sat down at my desk, and for some odd reason, I couldn't keep my eyes off of him. I felt like I was somewhat mesmerized.

I know what you're thinking, "Mesmerized in eighth grade? Yeah right." I'm probably exaggerating at this point, but I was surely lusting (*smile*). I continued checking him out. I noticed he had a cast on his arm. I was curious about what happened, but we never spoke that day.

The next day, I saw him again as expected. This particular day, we had to work with a partner to complete an assignment. I was still considered the "new girl", so I didn't have a preference regarding my working partner. I ended up working with another classmate. When the assignment was complete, I headed back to my desk. I opened my notebook just to find a white piece of paper that read, "Larry". It also had a phone number written below the name. I asked my peers, "Who is Larry?" No one responded. So, I threw the piece of paper on the ground. I heard a voice say, "I'm Larry." I turned around and it was the same African American guy, with straight back braids, who wore glasses. I began to smile. I went to pick the paper back up. He asked, "Are you going to call me?" I said, "Maybe."

I called him that night, and we talked for hours. I'll never forget he sung "With you" by Chris Brown. I couldn't stop blushing. He also told me about the accident that caused him to be paralyzed in his right arm. I opened up about being in foster care and why I'd always been embarrassed to tell others. He told me there is nothing to be embarrassed about because my story is what sets me apart from others.

Tip #3: Never be ashamed of your truth.

From that day forward, we promised to keep in contact no matter what happened. We talked on the phone everyday for about three weeks as friends. Then, he suggested that we take our friendship to the next level. We began dating, and the worst thing happened one week later forcing us to break up.

The Down Spiral
. . . .

There was a half of day at school, which meant classes were shorter. Although it was a short day, the expectation for me was to report back to the alternative school once my two classes ended. I decided not to go back to the alternative school. I believed if I stayed, I could spend more time with Larry. That wasn't the case at all. Larry had gone to class, and I sat in the library with my classmate who was also skipping. At the end of the school day, I called the group home and told Mrs. Jane I missed the bus. She wasn't falling for my lie. She told me that she'd already been in contact with transportation and the alternative school. An immediate meeting was called. It was decided that I would no longer be in transition at the public school due to a lack of trust. In addition, I was dropped down to the lowest level (*Bronze*), which consisted of no extracurricular activities at the end of the school day.

When I returned to the group home, I was also rendered consequences. I was put on restriction for one week, which consisted of no extracurricular activities, early bedtime, and no phone time. I couldn't be mad at anyone, but myself. However, I took my anger out on others. Another resident and I got into an altercation. It was on the verge of a physical fight if staff hadn't intervened. I got so upset that I stormed out of the group home. I wasn't thinking rationally at the time. Group home staff called the police and reported I had run away. I didn't consider storming out the house running away. I left the house to calm down. However, I was still convicted of violating my probation.

When police arrived, I had already come back. The officer told group home staff that since I had returned to the home, there was nothing they could do. The officer did give staff the option of going to the magistrate's office and taking a warrant out for my arrest. The officer left and everything seemed to have calmed down. At least, that's what I thought.

Around 2am, my sleep was interrupted by my room light and two police officers. I was shocked because I thought everything had truly calmed down. The officer said, "You have a warrant out for your arrest." I asked, "Why?" "You violated your probation," the officer replied. I then asked, "Am I being detained?" The officer said, "Yes, we'll be taking you to Durham Access." Durham Access was a mental health facility for adolescents and adults. I was brought in to be assessed overnight.

The next morning, I was seen by a clinician. The first question the clinician asked was, "Do you want to harm yourself or others?" I said, "No." He continued with a series of questions. He left the room once the assessment was complete. I didn't know why I was taken to a mental health facility in the first place. I thought, "People get into altercations all the time, but it doesn't make them crazy." But I've learned that foster children are always subjected to mental health issues just because we've experienced some form of "trauma", but hasn't everyone been exposed to trauma in some way?

When the clinician returned he said, "I don't believe there are any reasons to keep you here. You haven't shown any signs of harming yourself, and you've denied thoughts of harming others. I'm going to discharge you." I said, "Ok." I was released back to the group home.

When I walked in everything seemed out of place. Even the residents distanced themselves. It seemed as if everyone knew information that wasn't delivered to me. I walked to my room and sat on the bed. The group home staff member entered my room. She said, "Joshaline, you need to pack your things because you're moving." I looked at her and exclaimed, "MOVING! When did this decision come about?" She said, "I'm not sure. I'm just doing what was asked of me." I said, "Ok."

I had moved around so much that packing my things became a norm. It didn't bother me anymore. It got to a point where I didn't completely unpack my things when I moved. I had this preconceived notion that no matter where I moved, it wouldn't last long. The next day, Ms. Fantasia arrived at the group home. She explained that due to the significance of events that occurred, it was imperative that I be moved to a different placement. She believed that if I was moved to a new environment things would potentially improve.

Before moving to my next placement, I stayed in respite care for four days until a bed was available at the new group home. When the day arrived for me to move, I was prepared to take on the new journey.

New Directions

. . . .

I walked into the new group home, and I couldn't help, but notice there were no doors on the rooms. Every group home is run differently. So rather than complaining, I adapted to the living conditions. The group home director was present when I moved in. He welcomed me to New Directions Group Home. He also gave me a handbook of client rights and rules. I was given a tour by the other residents and shown my room. I settled in well.

The next day, a sheriff showed up to the group home requesting to speak with group home staff. After speaking with

with staff, the sheriff spoke with me regarding my recent probation violation. The sheriff said, "You'll need to show up to court due to the violation." I said, "Ok." He gave my court papers to staff.

When the day arrived for court, I wasn't sure what was going to take place. It seemed as though anytime I was optimistic, my hopes were shattered. So, I was thoroughly prepared for the worst. When my case was presented to the judge, the prosecutor desired the maximum sentence, which was to serve seventy-two hours in the juvenile detention center. My public offender advocated that I only serve twenty-four hours. He also emphasized that I was a talented young lady, and I was exposed to many things growing up. The judge asked, "What is your talent?" I said, "I write poetry."

Poetry was something that allowed me to express myself in a positive way. I was always good with words (*smile*). The judge agreed that if I recited the poem, I'd only be ordered to serve twenty-four hours in the juvenile detention center. So, that's what I did. The poem went a little something like this...

Rainbow

There's a rainbow in the sky to remind me of his love,
The love that God showers down from above,
There's a rainbow in the sky to remind me of his peace,

The peace that helps me cease my troubled mind,
Even when I have problems that I can't define…
I wish I remembered the rest of the poem, but unfortunately I don't. I was ordered to report to the juvenile detention center following my therapy appointment.

When the time arrived to turn myself in, I wasn't bothered at all. I actually went to the gate, pressed the button for assistance, and walked in calmly. I chuckled with group home staff while walking in, which wasn't the best idea. The processing clerk asked, "How much time is she ordered to serve?" I said, "Twenty-four." Before I could finish saying "hours", she told me to speak when spoken to. In that moment, I felt rage come over me. Although I wanted to curse her out, I remained calm. The group home staff member said, "I'm not sure." The processing clerk said, "Ok, I'll find out." The group home staff member left. I was put into a holding cell.

After I was completely processed, the officer performed a body cavity search. The most violating thing was I had to bend over and cough. I felt exposed and disgusted. Shortly after, I was taken to the shower. Before getting in the shower, I was given an antibacterial chemical for my hair. I gave the clerk the nastiest look imaginable. "Is there a problem?" she asked. I exclaimed, "Yes! Is this required?" She said, "Yes, it's protocol." I rolled my eyes. I was beyond angry because I didn't want chemicals in my hair, and I'd just gotten my hair done. My fresh doobie wrap was **POPPING** (*the modern word for super cute*). When I got out of the shower, I was given under garments and a jump suit two times my size. Then, I was escorted to my cell.

When I walked in the cell, I didn't have a mattress or covers. I was given a mat, a sheet, and magazines. It was **extremely cold**. They made sure you were uncomfortable as possible. Once the door shut behind me, I thought about everything I should've done differently and how I got to this point in my life. I had all the time in the world. Being in solitude was no fun, but I believed that was exactly what I needed. I counted every line on the wall, recited every poem that came to mind, and identified every car I could see through the tiny window just to pass time. I was restless and uncomfortable. It seemed as if the time was taking forever to pass.

At 5am Saturday morning, the detention officer woke me up and allowed me to take a shower. I was able to put my regular clothing back on since I was scheduled to be released later in the day. However, my time wasn't up until 3pm. So, there I was sitting in the cell once again. When 3pm did finally arrive, I couldn't think of a better time to appreciate my freedom. I never wanted to return to the juvenile detention center ever again.

When I got back to the group home, I made up in my mind that I wanted to do things differently. As I've always said after any major occurrence. I began taking my therapy sessions more seriously, holding myself accountable, and maintaining my behavior. This positive phase of my life lasted for several months, but ended abruptly when the QP (qualified professional) and I got into an altercation at the group home.

One day, I came home and new rules were implemented. That wasn't a surprise. However, I openly expressed my feelings about the new rules. The QP overheard me and came in my room to redirect the behavior. I was offended, and there the altercation sparked. I got up to walk out of the house, and she blocked the door. As any adult would because it was dark outside. I'm sure she was concerned with my safety. When she blocked the door, I asked her to move several times. She didn't move. I felt rage come over me. I pushed the QP out of my way in retaliation. She tried to restrain me, but it made things much worse. She struggled with taking me down to the floor, so she called another staff member for assistance. The staff member came to help her. She asked me to calm down several times. At that point, I was beyond angry. Once I became enraged, it was hard for me to calm down. I didn't care what anyone was saying or doing. I briefly calmed down, so they would release me.

Once I was released from the restraint, I walked into the living room. I flipped over all the furniture, causing the table to break. I then, stormed out of the group home. To my surprise, there was a sheriff waiting for me at the end of the driveway (*smile*). I was arrested and taken to Duke Hospital for a psychiatric evaluation.

When I arrived at the hospital, I still hadn't calmed down. When the nurse came in to ask demographic questions, I ignored her. I was then, escorted to my room. The nurse told me I was on suicide watch. I was required to give up anything that could potentially cause harm to me or others. This included my bra, jewelry, shoe laces, and my pony tail holder. I refused to give her anything. She gave me some time to make a decision. If I chose not to cooperate with her, she would take my things involuntarily. When she left, I thought about all the things that could potentially happen if I chose not to cooperate. So when she returned, I gave up everything. I was confident that I wouldn't be admitted to a psychiatric hospital because of prior evaluations. I assumed things would just calm down, and I would be discharged as I was in the past. Boy was I **WRONG**!

The next morning, I woke up to a sheriff sitting next to my bed. I looked around the room to ensure I wasn't dreaming. When the sheriff began speaking, I knew it wasn't a dream. She said, "Good morning, you'll be going to J.U.H." I asked, "What's that?" She said, "John Umstead Psychiatric Hospital." I exclaimed, "For what!" She said, "Baby, I'm just the person taking you. If you cooperate with me, I'll cooperate with you." I shook my head in disbelief. I guess my "not being admitted luck" expired. She proceeded to walk me to the car. Before getting into the car, she put me in handcuffs and shackles because I was labeled as a "runner". I rode confined for an hour and a half. **LET'S TALK ABOUT UNCOMFORTABLE!**

Visual Moment

I felt like my ancestors. They were forced to plank in handcuffs and shackles, confined for several hours. I could **NEVER** walk a mile in their shoes, but I felt like it that day!

It was the most unbearable ride you could ever imagine. I was convinced, the officer had put the handcuffs and shackles on as tight as she could. This resulted in bruises on both my wrists and ankles.

When I arrived at the hospital, I sat in the processing room for hours. We arrived during the morning, and I wasn't placed on a ward until late that evening. Each ward was based on the severity of the patient. I was placed with patients who were said to be "suicidal or homicidal". According to hospital staff, individuals who were admitted to the hospital stayed for an extended time period. However, my stay was short. I was in the hospital for six days. I made it clear to staff and the psychiatrist that I didn't react to the group home QP due to homicidal ideation, but as a result of her not allowing me to leave the home. I let them know that I wasn't crazy, and the decisions I made were my personal choices. There weren't voices in my head telling me to act on anything. The multidisciplinary team had a meeting and agreed I was ready for discharge.

Following my discharge, I went back to New Directions Group Home. Within that same week I had a permanency planning action meeting (PPAT). During the meeting, we discussed a reward system. My team believed it would assist with getting me off the path of self-destruction. This particular meeting felt different from any other one. Ms. Fantasia told me that Ms. Sonya from Columbia, South Carolina had been in contact with her regarding the possibility of adoption. I was beyond excited. I knew when I met Ms. Sonya she would be a wonderful mother if given the opportunity. Ms. Fantasia asked, "Is adoption something you desire?" I yelled, "YES!" in excitement. All I could think about was permanency. I spent majority of my life being moved around to different foster placements, so I desired a permanent home.

My social worker told me that she would begin the interstate compact paperwork. The interstate compact on placement for children (ICPC) is a process to ensure the adoptive placement of a child is in compliance of laws in both states. However, this process could take anywhere from six months to one year to complete. She told me that in the meantime, work on stabilizing my behaviors and effectively managing my anger.

During that time frame, my behaviors stabilized. I obtained the highest level (*platinum*) again at the alternative school. I successfully completed my intensive therapy program, and the greatest thing happened! I had six more months left to complete my probation, but the judge had received such great report. So, she dismissed the case early. I was well on my way!

It was the end of my ninth grade year. So much had taken place since eighth grade. It felt as if time was moving at the speed of light. I couldn't believe that I completed my first year of high school. After one year, the interstate compact was finally approved. It seemed like the perfect timing. My teachers gave me a going away party because I wouldn't be returning the next year. When I got home from school, I packed all of my things. Therefore, I would be ready for departure the next day. Of course, I couldn't sleep because I was so excited. All I could think about was being free from such a structured environment.

The next morning, Ms. Sonya arrived, and we headed to Columbia, South Carolina. My group home journey was finally over. At least, that's what I thought.

CHAPTER FOUR

THE PLOT TWIST

We finally arrived in Columbia, South Carolina, a place I could call home. I settled in well. Ms. Sonya, who I referred to as mom purchased my first cell phone. As you can imagine, it was an exciting day. My mom was also a foster parent. Therefore, I was able to interact with other teenagers. I felt like a normal teenager for once. I went to the movies with my friends, attended sleepovers, and had my own cell phone. Things seemed to be going in my favor. There were times my mom and I had disagreements, some worse than others, but we managed to get through it.

The school year quickly approached. My mom took me to register for classes at my new school. She also took me school shopping. I was a rising sophomore. I didn't know what to expect out of a large school because the alternative school was a small, personable environment.

On the first day of school, I was able to find my classes successfully. I met new friends, but the only thing that made me feel a bit uncomfortable is other children knowing my mom was a foster parent. Foster care was still the embarrassing part of my story that I didn't want others to know. In the past, I'd been teased and talked about simply because I was a foster child. Therefore, I preferred that no one knew. Other than that everything seemed to be going well.

Mid-semester had come quickly. I wasn't worried when grades were given out. As expected, I did well. However, I made my mom aware that I struggled in Spanish. I made 3A's, 2B's, and 1F. The ironic thing about my Spanish grade was my mom spoke it fluently. So, there were no excuses for failure. My mom gave me a pass for my grade, but expected me to pull it up as soon as possible.

A few weeks after grades came out; I met a guy who played football in my science class. I'd been eyeing him for awhile, but I was never the initiating type. He was handsome, chocolate, and athletic. He was definitely my type of guy. We were friends for a little while, but decided to take things to the next level. So, we made our relationship official. Well of course, the news spread around the school that "Joshaline was dating Joseph", and the drama began. Another girl who was in my class liked Joseph as well. Her name was Mary. To my surprise she rode my bus, and we lived in the same neighborhood.

One afternoon, I got on the bus to head home. Mary sat a couple of seats behind me. I overheard the girl talking about her disapproval of me and Joseph's relationship. Without thinking rationally, I turned around in my seat. I asked her, "Do we have a problem?" She said, "No, but we can." In that moment, I felt rage and reacted once again. I ran to her seat and began hitting her continuously. The driver stopped the bus. Some of the students on the bus intervened to stop the fight. I couldn't believe I fought her over a guy.

Tip #4: Never fight over a male or a female. Most of the time, the people we date in high school aren't our final destination anyway (*smile*).

When I got home, I didn't tell my mom about the fight. I assumed she wouldn't find out. The next day, I was pulled out of my first period class regarding the incident. The principle let me know he saw the recording of the fight. I had no idea cameras were on the bus. Due to the physical fight, I was suspended for eight days. The principle called my mom to inform her about the suspension. She was livid. She wanted to speak with me regarding the incident. When I got on the phone she asked, "Why didn't you tell me about the fight?" She then said, "You know I have to work. Now who is going to watch you while I'm at work?" I kept silent. I knew I'd screwed up, but it was nothing I could do at that point, but deal with consequences. She hung up the phone in disappointment.

When I got home from school, my mom spoke with me regarding the suspension. Due to the extent of the suspension and the minor disagreements, we agreed that I had more work to do before moving forward in the adoption. My mom called Ms. Fantasia to let her know what we decided. Within the same week, my social worker and GAL (guardian ad litem) was there to pick me up. I knew the chances of me finding a forever home was slim to none now. In regards to me and Joseph, you may as well say "our relationship ended" because I didn't hear from him after that day.

When I moved back to North Carolina, I went to a previous foster home. I began attending Southern High School. Ms. Reedy was happy to have me back, but I began displaying the same behaviors. I would run away from home, skip school, and my grades dropped significantly. I didn't care anymore. My foster mom believed she could no longer manage the behaviors. Therefore, I was moved to another foster home. This placement was out of the norm. I didn't see it coming at all, but I was definitely open to it. I moved in with the assistant principal of my high school. Ms. Davis and I connected when she caught me in the hallway play fighting with another student. She told me to go to class, and I caught an attitude with her. She called me to her office immediately. She asked, "What is your GPA?" I abrasively said, "I don't know." When she looked it up, I had a 3.2 GPA (grade point average). I guess that was pretty good for a tenth grader. She was thoroughly impressed. She asked, "Who are your parents?" I said, "I live in a foster home."

By the end of our conversation, she desired to be in contact with my social worker. She saw so much greatness inside of me, but I still hadn't realized my own. Ms. Davis welcomed me into her home. When I moved in with her, everything was going great as they always do in the beginning. I began improving my attitude, going to class, and pulling my grades back up, so my GPA wouldn't be heavily impacted.

One day I wanted to attend a party, and she didn't allow me to go. I went to the party without her approval. Ms. Davis decided that she wasn't going to tolerate that type of behavior. I pleaded her to stay, but her mind was made up. Her belief was, I'm a reflection of her. If she couldn't trust me to make positive decisions; I couldn't live in her home. I moved out a few days later. I was placed in respite care until my social worker was able to find a new placement. I told Ms. Fantasia about a previous foster home. I promised her that she wouldn't have any more problems out of me, if she allowed me to live there. I'd stayed at this specific foster home before for respite care, and she seemed like a cool foster parent. At least, that's what I thought. My social worker gave me a shot. As always, things started off wonderful and ended in shambles.

Ms Fantasia had enough! I believed that I gave her grey hairs at this point (*smile*). This entire time she catered to my request, but I was unappreciative of her diligent efforts. I had exhausted all the foster homes in Durham, North Carolina. Therefore, she decided that a children's home was the best option for for me. I was resistant when I was initially given the news. I told my team that I would intentionally get pregnant, so I wouldn't have to go. The children's home didn't have the resources at the time to accommodate pregnant residents. So, I thought it was a good idea. I also told them that I would run away and ensure they didn't find me. Let's just say…they made sure none of those things happened. I wasn't allowed to go anywhere unsupervised.

My best friend Larry was the exception because of the **HUGE LIE** that I told my foster mom. I asked her if Larry could come over. I told her that he was gay, so she wouldn't have to worry about anything potentially happening in her home. My foster mom allowed him to come over. Surprisingly when he came over, we all rode to the store together. This wasn't expected at all. During the ride, my foster mom said, "Larry, I heard you were sweet." Larry said, "I'm a sweet person. I would like to think so anyway." At that moment, I knew that I'd been caught in my lie. I began laughing to avoid feelings of awkwardness. My foster mom said, "No honey, Joshaline said, you were sweet as in go the other way." I burst out laughing to break the ice.

Visual Moment

Imagine your entire body going numb and you're unable to feel **<u>ANYTHING</u>**. This is what I was experiencing in this moment.

Larry exclaimed, "No, I'm not gay at all!" I admitted to lying about him being gay. I told my foster mom that I lied because I knew she wouldn't have allowed him to come over otherwise. My foster mom said, "You didn't have to lie. I would've allowed him to come over." I knew she was lying at that moment. However, I was happy that she allowed him to visit. Our last visit with each other was bittersweet, but as always we promised to keep in contact.

The next day, it was time for me to depart. Departing from my foster home was easy because my foster mom and I didn't get along that great. Ms. Fantasia and my GAL helped to pack all of my things in the car. After loading the car, we were in route to the children's home. I'd never been in a children's home before, so I asked my social worker tons of questions. The most important questions were regarding the name and the location of the home.

She told me it was called, "The Boy and Girls Homes of North Carolina." Additionally, she told me it was located in Lake Waccamaw, North Carolina. I yelled, "Lake WHO!" I'd never heard of such mysterious place in my life. She emphasized that it was three hours away from Durham, North Carolina, so I may not want to run away because it's an extremely rural place according to the research she had done. I began to laugh.

As we continued to ride, I thought about all I'd done, the many homes I disrupted, and how I needed to change. **FORREAL THIS TIME!** I was fed up with the way my life was going. I realized, I was my own setback, and the only one who could change that was me. I had always said in the past, "I'm going to change", but never followed through. I was exhausted with myself.

Tip #5: When you get tired of yourself, you know it's time for a <u>REAL</u> change.

I made a conscious decision that I wouldn't be the same person from that day forward.

CHAPTER FIVE

THE BOYS & GIRLS HOMES

We arrived at the children's home. The cottage director greeted us with a warm welcome. He escorted us to the cottage where I would be staying. When I arrived at the cottage, there were eight girls that came out to help unload my belongings. My teaching parents introduced themselves as The Hawthorne's. Teaching parents are the parental figures in the cottage. They showed me my room and introduced me to my roommate. They brought me into the office to go over the cottage rules, the point system, the dress code, and the daily schedule. They also let me know what I had on was inappropriate. Therefore, I was required to change my clothing after the meeting. I was wearing a spaghetti strapped shirt, a vest, and leggings. I wasn't allowed to wear anything revealing. My skirts had to be at least knee length, leggings were not allowed, shirts or pants couldn't have any holes in them, and all sleeveless shirts had to be at least three inches in width over the shoulder. I was convinced they wanted us to dress like the women in *Little House on the Prairie* (*smile*). However, modesty was a standard at the children's home.

The point system was another thing that my teaching parents emphasized. There were five levels. These included daily, weekly, negotiation, self-determination, and family life. Each level came with additional privileges. I asked, "Will I ever be able to hang out with my friends, have my own TV, or cell phone?" They said, "Yes, but those are privileges given to residents on higher levels." I then asked, "How long does it typically take for residents to reach the highest level?" They said, "It all depends on your progress." At that moment, all I could think about was purchasing my first cell phone. My mom had bought me a cell phone in the past, but it wasn't genuinely mines because I didn't purchase it. I wanted my own. So I kept my eyes on the prize, which was working the program for my benefit.

Within my first three months, I worked my way up to negotiation. Negation was the third level. When I had my first leveling meeting, Mr. Hawthorne said, "This person that we read about on paper isn't the person sitting in front of us. We worried about you when we found out you were coming to our cottage, but this is a totally different person." I smiled. When Ms. Fantasia heard the news, she was surprised. I guess she didn't believe I could make that quick of a turn around. Nonetheless, she was proud, but wanted to ensure I was getting everything I needed from the program. Therefore, she requested that I spend more time on each level. I was somewhat bothered by the decision, but I knew any decision she made was always in my best interest.

During the meeting, it was decided that I would attend the public school for the upcoming school year. I moved to the children's home towards the end of the school year. Therefore, I completed the remainder of tenth grade at the on-campus school. I'd always been on the university track. At the time, the on-campus school only offered a total of twenty-two credits. I needed twenty-eight credits to be admitted into a university. So, I was excited about attending the public school. It also gave me the opportunity to escape my reality and experience normalcy.

After the meeting adjourned, I was all the more motivated to work the program. Within the next three months, I was moved up to self-determination and to the pre-independent cottage. Residents who lived in the pre-independent cottage were held to higher standards. Some privileges were different as well. These included a later bed time, more phone time, and visits at the other cottages. I was appreciative of the extra privileges that came with self-determination and living in the pre-independent cottage. However, I kept my eyes on the **true prize**, which was to reach the highest level (*family life*).

My Internship Experience

· · · ·

The summer flew by as it always seemed to do. I was in the eleventh grade. I had one more year until I graduated. So, I wasn't off the hook yet. My first semester of school went well. I met a great friend name Elizabeth, who later became my best friend. We kicked it off to a good start, but as any friendship it came with its trials. We met in Algebra class. We connected instantly because both of us had no idea what was going on in the class. Math was not our strong subject at all. During class, we would have random conversations or take naps to pass time. Thankfully, we ended the semester successfully because the odds were surely against us (*smile*).

The next semester, I took an advanced placement (AP) course, played soccer, and ran track. I was active in high school. I went to the regional and state competition with the track team in the 4x4 relay. I was a great asset to the team. Extracurricular activities helped to take my mind off my reality. So, I never turned down a good opportunity.

During my AP class, my teacher gave all of her student's information regarding a summer paid internship. I thought it was a great opportunity to gain needed skills. I discussed it with my teaching parents. They told me that I would need to speak with the cottage director. After speaking with the cottage director, she gave me approval to submit my application. I completed the application and had three staff members submit references on my behalf. I gave the application my best effort. The next day, I put my application in the mail.

Towards the end of the school year, I was notified via mail. I opened the letter and in bold print it read, "**Congratulations you have been conditionally accepted into the North Carolina Community Development Initiative Program**." I leaped for joy.

When I got back to the cottage, I delivered the news to my teaching parents. They were happy for me. The letter gave me all the more drive to end my eleventh grade year successfully. So, I did just that!

I was finally headed to Raleigh, North Carolina for my internship orientation. This was the first time The Boys and Girls Homes allowed a resident to be a part of an internship opportunity. So, this was major. Although my trainings were held in Raleigh, North Carolina, I interned in Whiteville, North Carolina at the Columbus County Dream Center. The Dream Center is a non-profit organization that offers an array of programs to the community. As an intern, I worked with the summer camp program and aided staff with evening events. The director allowed me to accept this opportunity because he believed it would give me the proper networking exposure, gain independent living skills, and help to maximize my full potential. I thoroughly enjoyed the opportunity.

Towards the end of my internship, I told my supervisor that I desired a part-time job for continuous income. She took me to Food Lion and did a coaching with me before I went into the store. I got out of the car, took a deep breath, and walked in the store confidently. When I spoke to the manager, she was super nice. She told me that she was still hiring for cashiers, but I needed a youth workers permit because of my age. I was sixteen at the time. My supervisor took me to The Department of Social Services (*a place that was so familiar*) to get a workers permit. I took it back to the store. She told me I was hired and to come back in for training on Monday. I waited until I got outside to start leaping for joy. But boyyyy… when I did---I shouted (*a form of praise)* all the way to the car. I was so thankful. I got in the car and my supervisor said, "I can tell by your body language that you got the job." I yelled, "Yes, I got the job!" She said, "Congratulations." It was tough transitioning from my internship to Food Lion. I had become so attached to the staff, but they welcomed me back at any time.

Although things seemed to be going well, I still had my challenges. I felt the more time I spent at the pre-independent cottage, the more I was regressing. My teaching parents and I didn't see eye to eye on many things, but I managed my attitude well. However, for my sake it was best for me to be moved. Of course, that would take some time. At least, that's what I thought.

At my next leveling meeting, my team was actually

impressed with my growth, which wasn't what I expected. I guess it's true when they say, "We are our worst critic."

Tip #6: Don't sweat the small stuff.

I was moved up to the highest level (*family life*). My team also decided that it was an appropriate time for me to move to the independent cottage. God surely answered my prayers. I was ready to move out of the pre-independent cottage. They assured me that no one is perfect, and we all have unforeseen challenges that arise. It's how we deal with adversity that builds character.

After the meeting adjourned, I packed my things in preparation for the move. I moved into the independent cottage before the start of my senior year. The Richburg's were the teaching parents for the independent cottage. I would describe The Richburg's as a devoted couple who honors God in everything they do, effective disciplinarians, prayer warriors, and passionate about working with at-risk youth. The first time I met the Richburg's, there was an instant connection. I felt they understood me in a way that was different from others. So, I knew that I would thrive.

When I arrived, the Richburg's gave me the rules of the cottage and their expectations of family life residents. I settled in well. Now that I was finally on the highest level, I was able to buy my own cell phone and TV for my room. It was the most rewarding moment that I'd experienced in a long time. I felt accomplished. It gave me a jump start to my senior year. I knew my senior year wouldn't be the same because most of my friends graduated and went off to college. However, I managed to make the best of it. I met new friends and began dating a guy name David. He graduated a year ahead of me. We did a lot of talking over the phone, until we could physically see each other. He wasn't the type of guy that I would typically date, but he won my heart.

During my senior year, I maintained the A/B honor roll. I was given the opportunity to take online courses through nova net. Nova net is an online program used to take courses at your own pace. In addition to my standard classes, I was able to complete five online courses. I also worked part-time at Food Lion. I would say that I maintained an appropriate balance between school, work, and my social life. At least, that's what I thought.

One day, I was called to the guidance counselor's office. My mind began to race of all the negative things she would need to speak with me about. I asked myself, "Will I graduate on time? Was a grade submitted incorrectly? Did I miss an important deadline?" I did all of that stressing, just for her to tell me, "Congratulations, you're one of the selected few who are eligible for early graduation." I said, "Really?" She said, "Yes." I asked, "Have you spoken with my teaching parents?" She said, "No, but I would be more than happy to let them know." I walked out of her office saying, "Thank you Jesus" repeatedly. I had no idea I was eligible for early graduation. Although I would have to wait until the end of the school year to "officially" graduate, I was thrilled.

When I arrived at the cottage, I ran in to ask Mr. Richburg had he heard from the guidance counselor. He said, "No, we've been in meetings all day." I told him to check the voicemail on the cottage phone. He checked it and began to smile. He said, "Joshaline, I'm so proud of you, but we'll need to run this by the cottage director to ensure this is something the home would approve." I said, "Ok." My social worker and GAL were scheduled to come the next day for my plan of care meeting. A plan of care meeting gives youth the opportunity to decide what their plan will be after turning eighteen. The goal of planning is to ensure youth are thoroughly prepared for the transition out of care. It worked out perfectly because not only would I be able to discuss my plan of care, but I would also be able to deliver the news about my eligibility for early graduation.

The next day everyone arrived for the meeting. The meeting began with all of my major highlights (i.e. grades, behavior, the transition to the new cottage, etc.). Before discussing my plan of care, graduating early came up first. Ms. Fantasia said, "I don't have a problem with Joshaline graduating early. However, what will she be doing during that time?" The cottage director concurred. Mrs. Richburg gave the idea of taking courses at the community college during school hours because it would look good on my college application.

Therefore, the plan was I would attend Southeastern Community College during the day and work my part-time job at Food Lion after school. If there were days that I didn't have classes, I was expected to work at the on-campus food room. I was more than happy with the plan. In regards to my plan of care, I would be attending college when I turned eighteen. However,

I would still need some additional support. Therefore, it was in my best interest to sign the C.A.R.S agreement on my eighteenth birthday. The C.A.R.S agreement (Contractual Agreement for Continuing Residential Support) allows youth to stay in care until the age of twenty-one to receive additional supports and services. It gives youth the opportunity to gradually come into adulthood, rather than an abrupt transition.

After the meeting adjourned, I prepared my mind to take college courses and work every day instead of getting dressed in ugly uniforms to attend high school. During my last week of high school, I participated in free college application week. I applied to North Carolina Central University (NCCU), North Carolina Agricultural and Technical State University (A&T), and Winston Salem State University (WSSU). I knew that I wanted to attend a historically black college. My first choice was A&T because I heard so much about their school pride and homecoming experience. That shouldn't have been the only reason why I desired to attend A&T, but I was young.

Tip #7: Do your <u>research</u> before making a decision.

I didn't necessarily have a second or third choice because my heart was set on A&T. However, I received my first acceptance letter from NCCU. It wasn't the school of choice, but I wanted to take the opportunity of a campus tour just in case.

I began attending Southeastern Community College and working after school. I hadn't heard anything back from A&T or WSSU as of yet. According to some of my friends that went to A&T, it took them awhile to receive acceptance letters. So, I didn't get too discouraged. I remained patient and believed that what's for me, will be for me.

In the mean time, I went on college tours to NCCU and A&T. NCCU had a beautiful campus with a lot to offer, but I was from Durham, North Carolina. I didn't want to attend school in my hometown. On the other hand, A&T was truly an experience. The culture was something I'd never experienced before. I didn't want to attend any other school. Therefore, I contacted a great mentor of mine who was close friends with the admissions director. I truly believed that when there's a will, there's a way. She was able to advocate on my behalf. I received an acceptance letter via my application portal that same week. This was a prime example that it's not all about what you know, but who you know.

I was grateful and excited to be officially accepted into THE ILLUSTRIOUS North Carolina A&T State University. **AGGIE PRIDE**!

One day, I was randomly surfing A&T's website and came across a summer program opportunity. As I've stated, "I never turn down a good opportunity." The program would allow me to take my foundation math and english courses, which would ultimately put me ahead. I looked over the qualifications and saw that I was the perfect match. I discussed the opportunity with my teaching parents. They gave me approval to submit my application. If accepted, I would begin the program the day after my college orientation. As usual, I gave the application my best effort. I would receive a notification if I was accepted or rejected via mail.

A few weeks before my official high school graduation, I found out that I was accepted into the summer program. I was super excited! Not only was I accepted into the summer program, but I ended the semester at Southeastern with a 3.5 GPA. Everything was coming into place, until I received some terrible news.

My sister called the cottage to speak with me. I hadn't heard from her in what felt like ages. I never used the cottage phone, which was a red flag. I assumed this was her only way of contacting me. She sounded like something was bothering her. I asked, "What is wrong?" She said, "Our grandma is dying." In that moment, I didn't know how to feel. I felt emotionless. I hadn't heard from my grandmother since the day we left her home. Now all of a sudden she's dying. I was confused. I had so many questions, but of course my sister didn't have all of the answers. I asked her, "What do you mean she's dying?" She said, "Her body is shutting down." I hung up the phone. I needed time to process the information.

The next week, I tried to prepare for graduation without thinking about my grandmother. It was extremely hard. I took my graduation pictures and sent out invitations. I was limited to who I could invite because all guest were required to have tickets. I couldn't believe I sent a ticket to my biological mom because we didn't have a relationship. However, I respected her because she gave me life.

Tip #8: Even if your parents haven't been in your life as they should, the least you can do is give them respect for given you life.

I was able to invite all the important people in my life at the time. I coordinated with my social worker a day and time to go visit my grandmother before she passed.

When the day arrived, I was on edge. I thought, "What would I say to her? How would I react? Who else would be there?" When I walked in the hospice facility, it smelled like death and rotten flesh. It was the foulest odor ever. I signed in and walked to my grandmother's room. When I entered, I tried to remain calm as possible. I saw her lying on the bed with oxygen cords in her nose. I walked up to her bed and said, "Hey grandma, it's Ja-Ja (*my childhood name*)." She was unresponsive. I showed her my graduation picture and placed it on the side of her bed. I reached down to hug her. She tried to hug me back, but was too weak. That was a great indicator that she recognized me. It made me feel good on the inside. She let out a deep breath, and I'll never forget the scent of it. I sat with her for a few hours before saying my goodbyes. From the looks of things, she wouldn't make it much longer. I told her everything that happened since I left her home. I forgave her for everything that led up to me and my sibling entering foster care. I gently kissed her forever and exited the room.

One week later, my grandmother passed away. I wasn't able to attend her memorial service, which was a harsh reality. That hurt more than anything else, but I knew she was in a better place. She no longer had to suffer. I had to move forward, but I knew that time would heal all.

The Big Day

. . . .

The day I'd been waiting for all of my life finally arrived. As I put on my cap and gown, I thought about all it took to get to this day. I blew my own mind. When it was time for students to walk across the stage, I felt butterflies in my stomach. The first row was called, then the second, and then it was my row. My name was called, "Joshaline Yvonne Douglas." If I didn't have it together by then, this was my only shot. I looked down to make sure my gown was fixed properly. I tightened my cap up a bit and headed for the stage. I walked across the stage in confidence. I had one major milestone down and many more to go.

When graduation came to an end, I picked up my official diploma and headed outside to take pictures. To my surprise, my biological mom was waiting outside for me. It was awkward, but I was happy to see all of my family and friends. They truly made it a special occasion. Although I wished for that moment to last forever, it was time to depart and take on another journey in my life.

The Boys and Girls Homes provided the stability I needed to make the permanent changes in my life. They helped me to change the negative things that I believed about myself. Their commitment to my success was unwavering, and there will never be a moment to go by that I'm not thankful for The Boys and Girls Homes of North Carolina. I'll never forget the abundance of lessons learned while living there.

CHAPTER SIX

THAT UNFORGETTABLE MOMENT

Being dropped off to college was such a liberating, yet nerve racking experience. I had become so accustomed to being told when and how to do things, that I became a poor decision maker. However, it was time for me to learn how to make rational decisions. At least, that's what I thought. I believed coming to the summer program would give me the freedom that I so desired, but that wasn't the case at all. It was a structured, fast-paced program. It was solely about academics and completing the program successfully.

During the program, I made new friends and built strong relationships with two of the staff members, Aquanetta and Ms. Macfoy. Aquanetta would tell me that she saw a lot of herself in me. As we got to know each other, I found out that we shared similar stories. Our stories connected us all the more. Ms. Macfoy also saw a lot of potential in me. She was one of the counselors who advocated on my behalf because she saw past the exterior. I refer to these two women as my ride or dies because no matter what happened they always had my back!

Throughout the program, I struggled with time management. It seemed like I could never be to class on time, which was an expectation in the program. When I didn't make it to class on time, there were always sit downs with program staff regarding the expectation. The way my attitude was set up, I wasn't as receptive as I should've been. I was on strike number two, and the program was nowhere near being over. As I've always been told, "Three strikes and you're **OUT!**"

One night, there was a dorm room party being held on the third floor. Although we were in a summer program, other programs and students occupied the dormitory. Some of my colleagues and I decided to attend the party. When we walked in, we were given shots of alcohol. I thought I was grown (*smile*). I never tasted liquor before this particular day. I was fearful of the after effects. As the party continued, my head began spinning. I got up to walk to the air conditioner in the common area. I figured I needed to get some air because of all the body heat in such small space. It was extremely hot. I saw people leaving the room. I looked around to see if I'd seen any familiar faces. One of my good friends Madison, I met while in the program was the only person I recognized. She walked up to me and said, "Dr. Cox is looking for us." Dr. Cox was the program director. I remember running down the stairs and passing out. I woke up in Madison's room to the paramedics asking if I was okay. I was fine, but Dr. Cox recommended that I be taken to the hospital for precaution purposes. After medical evaluation, doctors believed my drink was potentially spiked, but assured that I would be fine. I was released from the hospital and headed back to the dormitory.

The next day, Dr. Cox contacted my social worker and delivered the news. I was dismissed from the program due to the extent of the incident and previous behavior concerns. After the down spiral of events, I was disappointed in myself. There I was being removed from something else. I thought I'd put those things behind me, but it was apparent that I needed more work in some areas. Ms. Fantasia picked me up the next day. She took me to another foster home for the remainder of the summer. During that time, I reassessed my growth areas and worked to improve them. I found out that I could be permanently suspended from the university due to the incident that occurred. I was worried, but I knew this couldn't be the end.

The judicial hearing was held a week before my official move-in day. All students that attended the dorm party were in the judicial hearing. The facilitator spoke to us about the importance of integrity. She also emphasized that drinking under age comes with a significant risk. There were parents in the meeting pleading for their children to receive another chance because some of them were seniors. The facilitator decided to give us all another opportunity under conditions. The conditional agreement was to complete a six week Alcoholic Anonymous (AA) program offered by the university. I couldn't participate in any extracurricular activities for a six-month probationary period. Although I didn't feel as if I needed to attend an AA program, I agreed for the sake of my educational endeavors. This will forever be that unforgettable moment.

CHAPTER SEVEN

A GLIMPSE OF COLLEGE

A week had gone by so fast! It was time to move into my dormitory. Ms. Fantasia picked me up from my foster home, and we headed to A&T. When we arrived, ironically I was in the same dormitory. My dorm room was four doors down from my previous room. The other great thing was David and Elizabeth stayed right down the hall. David was a resident assistant, which meant he had his own room. I knew his room would be my ultimate hang out spot.

Once we had everything moved in and set up, Ms. Fantasia gave me a hug and told me to do well. One thing about my social worker was she never gave up on me. She saw my potential and kept pushing me to bring it to fruition. After my social worker departed, reality set in. I was really on campus by myself, with no one to tell me what to do. Although I had David and Elizabeth as support, it was still a scary transition. However, I managed to find my way.

"Fresh Meat"

. . . .

I was seventeen years old when I began college, so there wasn't much I could do. I was referred to as an "Aggie pup" because I wasn't eighteen. There were times I used my friend's identification card to get in clubs and social gathering, but most of the time it wasn't worth it. Coming to college and initially being limited to social activities worked in my favor. I focused more on school. So when I did turn eighteen, my academic habits didn't change.

Around the third month of school, I received my refund check. I'd never received that much money. I always said, "When I get my first refund check, I'm going to buy a car." I was tired of driving David's car around, but he didn't mind. Before buying a car, of course I needed a license. That was the challenge.

David and Elizabeth worked with me for months on my

driving skills. When I went to take my first driver's test, I failed. According to the licensing agent, I took off too fast and didn't back up properly. Although those things were true, I was beyond upset. I had to wait a whole week to retest. During that time, I consistently practiced. When I went back the second time, **I PASSED** (*smile*). So, I finally purchased my first car. It wasn't anything spectacular, but it was mine. I treated my dodge neon as if it was a foreign car. I also obtained my first job as a freshman. I worked at Body Central, a retail store for women. I could've transferred to a Food Lion in the surrounding area, but there were no openings. So, I decided to let that job go.

By the time I looked up, the semester was over. I ended my first semester with a 3.76 GPA. I was elated! I completed all the requirements of my probation. I could finally be active on campus. Before proceeding to do so, I went to speak with Ms. Macfoy about rejoining the TRIO program. Being that I was dismissed from the summer program, it also dismissed me from the TRIO program. TRIO is a federally funded program that serves and assists low income individuals, first generation students, and individuals with disabilities. This program offered beneficial services, which is why I desired to be apart. Ms. Macfoy advocated on my behalf, and I was readmitted to the program. I couldn't thank her enough. I didn't waste any time becoming active on- campus. I joined Verge Modeling Troupe. I participated for one semester and gave it up. I was tired of my feet hurting every day (*smile*). Additionally, I noticed that the more involved I became on-campus, the more networking I did with others.

Well one day, I was leaving out of the student union and a guy literally ran up behind me. He introduced himself as Christian. He told me he'd been watching me for a while. It sort of freaked me out. I couldn't help, but to blush because he was so handsome and smelt amazing. Once again, lusting after something I knew wasn't right (*smile*). He asked for my phone number, which was a conflict of interest because I was in a relationship. However, I gave him my number anyway. That probably wasn't the best idea, but we all shoot our shot (*smile*).

We hung out a couple of times and nothing ever happened, but I was pushing my luck. However the last time we hung out, it didn't end as expected. We became intimate with each other. I couldn't lie to my boyfriend, so I told him what happened. He was furious, but he forgave me. Although things seemed to improve, our relationship took a major shift.

Nonetheless, I ended my freshman year with a 3.70 GPA. I decided to attend summer school because it was a way to get ahead. It would also give me a place to stay during the summer months. Although I signed the C.A.R.S agreement, I didn't want to go to another foster home. I spent my entire life living in different foster homes. Now that I had a choice, there was no way I was going to another one. Being that I never went, the foster parent contacted my social worker to let her know she wasn't willing to do the agreement anymore. Therefore it was switched to mom, which worked out better. I completed the summer session successfully. I was a rising sophomore.

Sophomore Year

* * * *

My sophomore year started off great until about mid-semester. I began having roommate problems. I was moved to a new dormitory because the issues had gotten so bad. Moving was the best decision, or things would've gotten ugly. To top things off, I went through an emotional break up with my boyfriend. It was totally my fault. Remember when I said, "Things seemed to get better." Well it didn't really get better. If anything, our relationship got much worse. He no longer trusted me. What's a relationship without trust? Sounds like a pointless relationship to me. Our relationship went down in shambles. It was a hard pill to swallow, but I knew things would get better with time. I accepted that he and I were no longer together. I would usually stay with his family during school breaks, but I stayed with one of my friends instead.

After spending break at her home, I realized I needed my own apartment. I was grateful she allowed me to stay, but I didn't want to continue having to find places to go. I spoke with my scholarship advisor from The Boys and Girls Homes. She let me know that The Boys and Girls Homes funded rent up to $500 a month. She asked, "Why hadn't you said anything sooner?" I said, "I didn't know, or I would've given roommates up a long time ago." I began telling her about my roommate issues, and how I had to find places to go during school breaks. She told me to find an apartment within the budget, but I would need to wait until the end of the school year to move. I had spring break to get through, and I would finally have my own place.

I didn't have plans for spring break, but I always figured.

things out. I started a new job at a hotel, working the evening shift. My first day was the same day spring break began. When my shift ended, no one showed up for the next shift. I worked two additional hours, and I left. I was fired for leaving the office unattended, but I had no idea where I would lay my head that night. I thought long and hard. My friend Jasmine came to mind. I called her at 1am, and she welcomed me in with open arms. I stayed there for the full week of spring break. She was my life saver. After spring break, I headed back to school. It always seemed as if the semesters flew by. I finished my sophomore year successfully, even through the emotional break up and roommate issues. Those issues were minor compared to some of the things I had experienced in the past. I thought, "What are a few issues to someone who has learned how to survive her entire life?" My response was "nothing" because I CAN CONQUER ANYTHING!

Tip #9: Always believe in yourself! If you never have anyone else, you always have yourself.

I moved into my apartment once the semester ended. I utilized LINKS services to assist with the necessities for my apartment. LINKS is a program that serves foster youth who are in care sixteen to eighteen and who have aged out of care eighteen to twenty-one. The program funded $500 for my apartment needs. That was one less thing I had to worry about. It felt good to be in my own space. I didn't have to worry about anyone stealing my personal belongings.

I took on the summer with full force. I got a new job at Victoria Secret. I enjoyed the job, but I rarely got hours. So, I quit. I had to do something fast because I wanted money. I enjoyed shopping and eating out way too much. I submitted numerous applications, but I never received any calls back. So, I took advantage of my summer, by spending time with family and friends. I reconnected with my biological mom, I found my long lost sisters on my father's side, and I caught up with my best friend Larry. Before I knew it, the summer was over. It was time to take on another year of college.

Junior Year

. . . .

My junior year was different from any other year. My life seemed to be less chaotic. At least, that's what I thought. After all the job applications I submitted, I finally landed a job at a daycare center. I liked the job because of the flexibility and working with children. I was able to work around my school schedule, which is hard to come by. I thoroughly focused on school my junior year. There were times I had fun, but academics came first. I was inducted into two honor societies. These included Phi Alpha Honor Society and Golden Key International Honor Society. I was thrilled.

Toward the end of the school year, I selected an internship to satisfy my curriculum requirements. Students were asked to choose three internships of interest. Therefore if one wasn't unavailable, another option could be accommodated. All of my options included working with at-risk youth. I was passionate about this population because I once was an at-risk teen. I thought, "What better way to give back to the community?" I landed an interview with Communities In Schools (CIS). Communities In Schools is a program that surrounds students with a community of support, empowering them to remain in school, and achieve in life. During the interview, I shared my personal story on how I had overcome adversity. The interviewing panel was thoroughly impressed, and I was selected for the internship. I ended my junior year out with a bang.

I officially began my summer. I worked at the daycare and dedicated myself to a healthier lifestyle. I began working out and meal prepping every day. My apartment had a gym, which was convenient. One day in particular, I went to the gym and got on the treadmill. A random guy came in the gym. I couldn't help, but notice him because he was handsome, chocolate, and athletic. He was definitely my type of guy (*smile*). We made eye contact on several occasions, but I wasn't the type to initiate anything. He walked up to me while I was on the treadmill. He said, "I've never seen you before; do you go to school around here?" I responded, "Yes, I go to A&T." He said, "Wow, me too. What church do you attend?" I said, "I don't have a church home at this time."

At that time in my life, I wasn't attending church on a regular basis. So I didn't necessarily have a church home, but I visited different churches in the area. He proceeded to invite me to his church. I thought, "What a great way to reel me in." We exchanged numbers, and the rest was history. Later on that day, he told me his name was Devon. He was a junior as well. We became great friends that quickly turned into something more. We had lot of fun together. We enjoyed similar things, so it made the relationship all the more interesting. We also held each other accountable in the gym.

Eventually, I stopped working out with him because he was extremely aggressive in the gym. It was almost like he wanted the work out more than I did. This led to me hiring a personal trainer. He didn't approve the idea of a trainer, but I got one anyway.

The next morning, my training sessions began. Devon popped up at the gym. I wasn't expecting him at all. I could tell by his body language he was upset and felt somewhat intimidated. He walked up to me and asked, "Is this your personal trainer?" I said, "Yes, but we can talk about this later." Once my training session was over, he and I spoke about the situation. He didn't feel it was necessary for me to hire a personal trainer because we had each other. I expressed to him that he was too aggressive in the gym, and I desired someone who was more patient.

The conversation ended with us breaking up. We only made it in a relationship two months. I was hurt, so I sought revenge. I told him that I wanted the $350 watch I bought him back. Of course, he told me no. I told him if he didn't give it back, I would press charges on him. I knew that I couldn't lawfully because I gave it to him as a gift, but I wanted to scare him. I tried calling and texting him several times, and he didn't respond. I happen to ride out to the store and spotted his car. We literally went on a high speed chase, but I lost him. A couple of days later, I received a random voicemail from a sheriff. I called the number back, and the sheriff explained he would need to come by my apartment to discuss matters in further detail. I was confused. When the sheriff arrived, he explained that Devon had filed a 50b against me. He left the paperwork with me and emphasized the upcoming court date. I couldn't believe it, but there was nothing I could do.

The day arrived for us to attend court. The judge called our case. When we came to the stand, the judge asked for Devon's side of the story first. Devon began telling the judge about how great our relationship was in the beginning. The judge quickly cut him off and redirected him to the reason we were in court. The judge asked probing questions regarding the incident. Once all the evidence was presented, the judge told both of us to grow up and dismissed the case. The incident was a terrible ending to my summer, but I refused to let it impact the start my senior year.

Senior Year

. . . .

I made sure my senior year was nothing less than amazing. I was more involved in social activities on-campus. I participated in every homecoming event, which I'd never done. A&T is known for its homecoming experience. It's literally the greatest homecoming on earth. **AGGIE PRIDE**! Mid-semester arrived in no time. They say, "Time flies when you're having fun." I decided that I wanted to continue my education in the field of social work. I applied to several graduate programs, but I was set on NCCU. It was the only school I knew of that offered an advance standing program in the evening. This meant I could work during the day. Advance standing is a fast-paced program that allows students to obtain their MSW (Masters of Social Work) in one year versus two. As usual, it took forever to hear back from any of the schools.

Spring break had come, and I went to Miami, Florida, which is the typical place for all students to go during that time. I had a blast! The day after I returned, I received a notification from NCCU. I checked my portal, and a decision had been made regarding my acceptance. I was nervous to open the letter, but I did anyway. When I opened it, the first thing I saw in bold words was "**Congratulations, you have been conditionally accepted into the North Carolina Central University advance standing social work program**." I dropped my phone, screamed, and ran around my apartment what felt like one hundred times. I was extremely excited! I put my all into the application, and my efforts had paid off. My expected date of graduation was May 14, 2016, and my MSW program was expected to begin on May 24, 2016. I didn't necessarily have a plan after graduation. After being accepted into the MSW program, I knew for sure I would be continuing my education. The other applications I submitted no longer mattered because I was accepted into NCCU.

The day had come for me to take senior pictures. It felt good being able to put on a cap and gown for a second time. This was another major milestone. I prepared myself for the big day to come. I had my invitations and pictures made on the same day. When I received them, I immediately went home and prepared to send them out the next day. Once all of my invites were sent out, I spent my last few weeks studying for my examination. I was exempt from all of my exams, except one. However, I passed that one exam successfully. I was inducted into two more honor societies. These included Chi Alpha Epsilon National Honor Society and Alpha Kappa Mu Honor Society. It was an honor to be acknowledged for academic success. When the week of graduation arrived, I picked up my honors chords, graduation identification badge, attended graduation rehearsal, and Saturday was graduation day.

Saturday morning, I was eager to get dressed and put on my cap and gown. I remember looking in the mirror and saying, "YOU GO GIRL!" Once I got dressed, I headed to the arena for graduation. I never knew a graduation to be so long. According to popular news, the Class of 2016 was the largest class of students graduating in the history of A&T. That was apparent because I sat for four hours before they called The School of Behavioral and Social Sciences. When it was my turn to walk across the stage, I had butterflies in my stomach as usual. I gave my identification badge to the graduation reader. When I heard "Joshaline Yvonne Douglas", I walked in confidence across the stage. It was literally the quickest ten seconds of fame, but it felt amazing. I didn't stay until the end of the ceremony. I met up with family and friends after walking across the stage. I was overwhelmed from all the support I received on my graduation day. I had accomplished so much in my past, but this one topped them all. I was prepared to take on my next journey, which was the most unexpected stage of my life.

CHAPTER EIGHT

SO UNEXPECTED...

Going to graduate school had always been a goal of mine, but I didn't think it would come so soon. I literally had two weeks to enjoy life without any academic responsibility. I partied hard every day for two weeks straight. I thoroughly enjoyed myself because I knew once school began, I wouldn't have that option. During that time, I decided to try something new. I "figured" it was time to start dating again, but this time I wanted to do things a little different. I joined an online dating site in hopes of finding "Mr. Right". I met a guy name Marcus. He and I hung out for awhile, and we decided to take things up a notch. We began dating, and the rest was history.

Those two weeks felt more like two days. It was time for

me to attend orientation. During orientation, staff emphasized that the program would be more challenging than our undergraduate studies. They said, "Don't be alarmed if you all see more B's than A's." I became nervous, but I knew that I could take on the challenge.

During the summer months, classes were held on Monday, Wednesday, and Friday. The first part of the summer session was challenging. Once it ended, I knew what my professors expected. So when the next session began, I excelled. I ended the summer session with a 3.5 GPA. I kept an open mind when it came to my grades. My goal was to pass. That probably wasn't the best mindset to have, but it got me through.

I was ready to take on the fall semester, but I had to identify an internship first. This was the hard part. Every place I had identified fell through, but all wasn't lost. I landed my internship at Duke Regional Hospital on the psychiatry unit. I was able to secure this internship through my prior social worker Ms. Fantasia. She was working on the unit at the time and spoke with her supervisor who offered me the opportunity. I finally secured an internship for the fall.

During the fall semester, classes were held on Tuesday,

Thursday, and Saturday. I never imagined sacrificing my weekends for the sake of academics, but I wanted a master's degree. Therefore, I did what needed to be done to successfully complete the program. As the semester progressed, I was more tired than usual. I began missing Saturday classes, which was a red flag because I take my studies seriously. I decided to take a deeper look into things. The first thing I assessed was my menstruation calendar. I was two days late for my period, which was normal because I had an irregular cycle. So, I didn't think anything of it. A couple of weeks passed, and my cycle still hadn't come on.

On August 27, 2017 me, Marcus, and his son went to the zoo. As we were walking, I experienced an unbearable sharp pain in my uterus area. At that point, I knew something was wrong. When I got home, I looked in the cabinet for a pregnancy test. Thankfully, there was one in there. I took the test, and blue lines surfaced immediately. **I WAS PREGNANT**!!! I starred at the test for about two minutes. I then, called Marcus in the bathroom to deliver the news. We both were silent for the rest of the night. I refused to accept that I was pregnant. I went to the store that night and bought two more pregnancy tests. When I took them, they also read positive. So many thoughts went through my mind,

"Do I have what it takes to be a good mother? Will I have the proper support? What if I have twins?" The list goes on. Bottom line, I wasn't ready to accept I was pregnant.

The next morning, I went to the women's hospital to see if I was in fact pregnant. The home pregnancy test wasn't convincing enough. The first question the nurse asked was, "Did you have a positive home pregnancy test?" I said, "Yes, but there is always a possibility it can be wrong." The nurse said, "You're pregnant, but I'll give you another test to confirm it." She gave me a cup to take a urine sample. After I gave her the sample, I went back to sit in the lobby until my name was called. A few moments later, I was called back. The nurse said, "Congratulations, you're five weeks and four days pregnant. I asked, "How are the weeks calculated?" She said, "Since we don't know the exact date of conception, we go by the last day of your menstrual cycle." I asked, "So in reality, I'm only two to three weeks pregnant?" She said, "Yes." In that moment, I smiled in excitement.

As I was leaving the hospital, I became emotional. I considered abortion, but I knew that would go against my personal values. I considered quitting school, but I had already begun the program. I had never been the type of person to start something without finishing. I came to the realization that with every decision, there are consequences. So, I put my big girl pants on and prepared to be a mother.

Tip #10: You do the "crime"; you do the "time". I put myself in the situation, and now I had to deal with the consequences to my poor decisions. It's life!

Fall semester went smoothly. However, the start of my internship was delayed due to unforeseen requirements. I was only required to work twenty-four hours a week, but I worked forty hours to ensure I satisfied all of my internship hours. Working on a psychiatry unit with adults that had severe mental illness, while pregnant wasn't a good combination. There were times I wanted to give up, but I kept my baby in mind.

Marcus and I were scheduled to find out the gender of the baby on November 28, 2016. However, our relationship ended before then. Therefore, we agreed to co-parent. It wasn't the ideal situation, but you live and learn. My child's father is a wonderful person, but I've learned that when you step out of the will of God, you connect with people who God didn't intend for you to be with. The same way that you connected with a person, is the same way you have to keep that person, which ran the risk of sacrificing my own happiness. I wasn't intended to be with him, and I accepted that reality.

The day arrived to finally find out the gender of the baby. He and I had names picked out for both genders, but I knew it was a boy. They say, "Mothers have a great intuition." The ultrasound specialist confirmed that it was in fact a boy. I told her that God knew just what I needed in this season of my life. After my doctor's appointment, I went shopping for my baby boy. It wouldn't have been me not to go shopping. I tried not to buy too many items because I was having a baby shower.

I announced to my immediate family and friends the gender of the baby. Many of them were hoping for a girl, but they were happy either way. I felt at that time it wasn't appropriate to announce my pregnancy on any of my social media platforms. At that point, I had wholeheartedly accepted my pregnancy, but I wasn't ready for the world to know. My priority at that time was completing school successfully and having a healthy pregnancy without being scrutinized. Although a hard task, I managed well. I ended the fall semester with success. I was proud of myself for pushing through, given the circumstances that occurred throughout the semester. I thoroughly enjoyed my winter break, but I knew when I returned people would question my developing stomach (*hence the significant weight gain*). I was willing to confirm that I was pregnant, but I didn't want it on social media.

When school started back, the strange looks began. My professor pulled me to the side and asked if there was something I needed to tell her. I told her that I was pregnant. Her mouth dropped in shock. She asked, "How in the world did you go the entire semester without telling me?" I said, "I wasn't ready for anyone to know." The majority of my friends in the program knew I was pregnant, but for those who didn't, I didn't hear the end of it (*smile*). People asked, "Did you eat too much for the holidays?" I politely said, "No, I'm pregnant and have been since the beginning of the fall semester." When I arrived back at my internship, I was also questioned about pregnancy. At that point, I let everyone know that I was pregnant and was expected to have a baby boy on April 27, 2017.

During spring semester, my classes focused solely on developing my final research proposal. I was also required to complete three hundred hours for my internship. I had a lot of work to do, but I was determined to get it done. My topic for my proposal was *"The Effects of Youth Aging Out and Identifying Appropriate Services."* This topic hit close to home because I had aged out of the foster care system. I utilized a qualitative method, which allowed me to interview individuals who had also aged out of the foster care system. It gave them the opportunity to share their experiences and services that would've been beneficial to them.

It was truly a rewarding experience. I was able to briefly tell my story and engage participants to do the same. After gathering all the imperative information, I developed my research proposal. Once completed, I was ready for my presentation. However, the week that I was scheduled to present was the same week that I could potentially go into labor. Therefore, my professor allowed me to present a few weeks early. My presentation went exceptional. It went way better then I imagined. I also satisfied the hours for my internship early. I felt accomplished when I completed everything. Now, my only task was to ensure a healthy delivery.

April 15, 2017, a day I'll never forget. I convinced myself that castor oil would induce my labor. I had watched multiple videos on YouTube of women who utilized this method. From my understanding, it only worked if the body was ready to go into labor. So, I took a shot at it and failed. I realized that I probably should be patient and not rush the process. I knew that I would miss him being on the inside when my pregnancy was over. My only desire was to deliver two weeks before my graduation ceremony. I wanted him to experience my special moment outside of the womb.

At my next appointment, I emphasized to my doctor the desire to deliver two weeks prior to graduating. I was forty weeks pregnant on the day of my appointment. The doctor asked, "Have you tried any natural remedies to induce labor?" I said, "I've tried everything within my means, but nothing seems to be effective." My doctor discussed it over with her colleagues. She agreed to induce my labor on the upcoming Friday, April 28, 2017. It was Monday, April 24, 2017, so I had four more days to go.

I went home and cleaned my entire apartment. Talk about nesting! I had everything packed for the hospital. I let his father and my doula know the day of my scheduled induction. I continued to walk, bounce on my exercise ball, dance to the "baby mama" song, drink raspberry leaf tea, and complain about how bad I wanted the baby out.

It took forever for my induction day to come. At least, that's what I thought. When the day finally arrived, my doula came to pick me up that morning. We stopped to get breakfast before going to the hospital because I knew they would put me on a strict diet. My child's father met us at the hospital. I was extremely nervous because as a first time mom, I didn't know what to expect. However, I was excited to meet him.

When we were escorted to the birthing room, I was put on a monitor. My nurse inserted an IV in my arm and a pill in my vaginal area to begin dilation. Within the first thirty minutes, I started having contractions. The contractions started off minor, but gradually became severe. My nurse came back to check my progress. She said, "You're progressing well." My friend Jasmine (*my life saver*) joined us in the birthing room as additional support. By the end of the day, I was four centimeters dilated. The contractions had gotten so intense that I requested an epidural. I heard so many negative things about the epidural, but I disregarded them all when the pain became unbearable. The epidural was given successfully.

Early Saturday morning, my water broke. I remember

yelling, "My water broke!" My child's father, my doula, and Jasmine all jumped up. I assumed it was go time, so I called the nurse. When the nurse entered the room, she realized my water was brown, which indicated the presence of meconium. Meconium is known as the first stool of an infant. So, my nurse inserted a monitor vaginally to observe his breathing. According to my nurse, meconium can cause great risk to a baby if it enters the lungs. However, she told me not to worry.

After the monitor was applied, I was able to sleep for a couple of hours. When I woke up, I was in excruciating pain. This time it didn't feel like contractions. It felt like he was pushing himself out of my bottom. I called the nurse for pain medication, but it only brought relief for a short time. This continued for several hours. I tried to get in numerous positions, but they were unsuccessful. The pain was so intense, I vomited. My nurse decided to check my cervix once more to see if I'd made any progress. I was still four centimeters dilated, which was extremely frustrating. I continued to bear the pain for several more hours, until I couldn't take it any longer.

My doctor came in and offered me a c-section because I wasn't progressing. It took me one minute to make a decision. I went with the C-section. Although not the ideal way to deliver, I wanted relief. The nurses came in to prepare me for the major surgery. I had a severe case of labor shakes. My child's father geared up for the C-section as well. Jasmine and my doula waited in the recovery room. The nurses rolled me back to the surgical room, lifted me off the hospital bed, and laid me on the surgical table. The doctor told me everything he was doing before he did it. He told me he was going to test the incision area to see if I was completely numb by pinching the skin. I felt the pinches, and realized I was only numb on one side. The doctor told nurses to give me a spinal tap, which consisted of them lifting me off the table again. I felt like I was going to pass out. I asked the nurses for oxygen, and my request was honored.

Once I was given the spinal tap, my doctor gave me another pinch test to ensure I was completely numb. I was still only numb on one side. The doctor then injected something in my IV. All I remember is going into a deep sleep. I woke back up to the nurses telling me my bundle of joy had arrived. I was emotional and exhausted. They rolled me to the surgical recovery room to check my incision and vital signs. I was able to finally meet my sweet baby boy, Noah Cameron. I fell in love with him the moment he was placed in my arms.

We were discharged after four days, due to him having jaundice. The first night at home was tough. I didn't get any sleep. I was so worried about my son. I heard a lot of information regarding SIDS (Sudden Infant Death Syndrome) and it scared me. He woke up every two hours to be breastfed, but overall he was a great baby. I made sure that I took my meds on time to stay ahead of the pain. I limped for the first couple of days. It felt like my guts were going to drop out of me at any moment. By the end of week one, I got into the swing of things. I was thankful for my family, friends, and his father who came to assist with the baby, but it was time to prepare to walk across the stage.

On May 8, 2017, I attended my graduation rehearsal. I also found out that I made all A's for the semester. I was extremely proud of myself.

May 13, 2017, had quickly approached. It was finally graduation day! I coordinated with my teaching parents; The Richburg's to watch Noah during graduation. As I prepared to walk across the stage, I reflected over my life, the good and the bad. I was reminded that there is always light at the end of the tunnel. Sometimes we have to go through, to get to, where God wants us to be. No matter what life seemed to throw my way, I was the author of my story. I dictate my ending. It's not all about where we start, but how we finish is what counts. Make your journey count! Through the twenty-nine foster homes that I couldn't capture in one book, the continuous school changes, and the multitude of adverse challenges, **I MADE IT**. With tears in my eyes, I gave the graduation reader my identification card, and walked across the stage with confidence. When I was hooded, I felt a burden lift off of my chest. I knew that I had truly conquered by building resilience.

Closing Remarks

• • •

Through my entire reservoir of experiences, I've learned that change cannot occur, until something occurs in us. I accepted that I wasn't dealt the best of cards in life, but was I going to allow it to stop me? No! I was tired of making excuses and setting goals, but not following through. We can't move forward in our lives by making excuses. A well known poem says, "Excuses are the tools of the incompetent, used to build bridges to nowhere, and monuments of nothingness." The same energy that we use to make excuses is the same energy that can be used to develop a plan, try something new, be creative in our thinking, or **be** the difference in the lives of others. I now understand that through my hope, it gave me the strength to realize that my purpose was far greater than my obstacles and everything that I went through was connected to my purpose. So, don't become weary in troubled times because everything has divine purpose. I challenge you to change your way of thinking and remember **YOU ARE RESILIENT!** Romans 12:2 (NKJV) states "And *do not* be conformed to this world, but be transformed by the renewing of your mind, that you may prove what *is* that good and acceptable and perfect will of God." I live by this scripture because there is no way I could've permanently changed without first renewing my mind.

CONCLUSION

Our lives don't necessarily have a conclusion because we're constantly evolving. However, I moved on to the next journey in my life. I've learned that each level in my life demanded a different version of me. I'm no different from anyone else who experiences adversity, but it's how we deal with such things that build character. Our stories are what separate us from others. Whether your story had all good moments or even some gray areas, each occurrence has contributed to the individuals we are today. Never be ashamed of your truth. Your truth has the power to help someone else. Believe it or not, adversity isn't always a bad thing. It demands us to learn, grow, and sow seeds in the lives of others. So step out on your dreams, have audacious faith, and trust your journey. Your journey is distinct; therefore don't ever compare it to others. As we go forward to embark the many adventures of life remember **YOU ARE RESILIENT**!

"YOU ARE **RESILIENT,**
YOU ARE **EXTRAORDINARY**"

DID YOU KNOW?

According to National Foster Youth Institue (2017),

- More than **23,000** children will age out of the foster care system in the US each year.

- After aging out at eighteen, **20%** of those youth will instantly become homeless.

- There is a **3%** chance for youth who have aged out to earn a college degree at **any point in their life**.

- **7 out of 10** girls who age out will become pregnant before the age of 21.

- In 2015, more than 20,000 youth failed to reunite with their biological families or find permanency after aging out.

- Only **1 out of every 2** foster youth who age out will obtain gainful employment by the age 24.

I beat <u>ALL ODDS</u>, and you can TOO!

MEET THE AUTHOR

Joshaline is originally from Durham, North Carolina. She's a social worker by trade, but a mother, speaker, advocate, change agent, and now an author by day. She has been a keynote speaker for several organizations such as Kiwanis International, The Kiwanis Key Club, Civitan International, The Women's Club, Victory and Jesus Ministries, and The Boys and Girls Homes of North Carolina. Joshaline's passion lies in the practice of social work.

Joshaline is a proud graduate of North Carolina A&T State University (NCA&T) and North Carolina Central University (NCCU). Joshaline is currently pursuing her PhD in Human Services at Capella University and is expected to graduate in September of 2021.

Outside of being a public figure, Joshaline spends most of her time taking care of her son and business planning. Joshaline hopes to be a professor in the near future and to open an independent living group home for at-risk young adults.

CONNECT WITH JOSHALINE

Let's Connect!

Any questions or comments about the book can be sent directly to joshaline.douglas@gmail.com. Or you can send a message through any of the social media platforms listed below.

Twitter: Joshalined

Instagram: Joshalined

SnapChat: Joshaline D

Facebook: Joshaline Douglas